ABC'S OF HORSES

A is for Appaloosa

An Appaloosa is a breed of horse which has a colorful, spotted coat pattern.

B is for bronc

A bronc is a wild or untamed horse used particularly in rodeo. They are bred for their feisty attitude.

B is for bay

Bay describes a horse with a brown body and a black mane, tail, and lower legs.

B is for buckskin

Buckskin describes a horse with a tan coat and a black mane, tail, and lower legs.

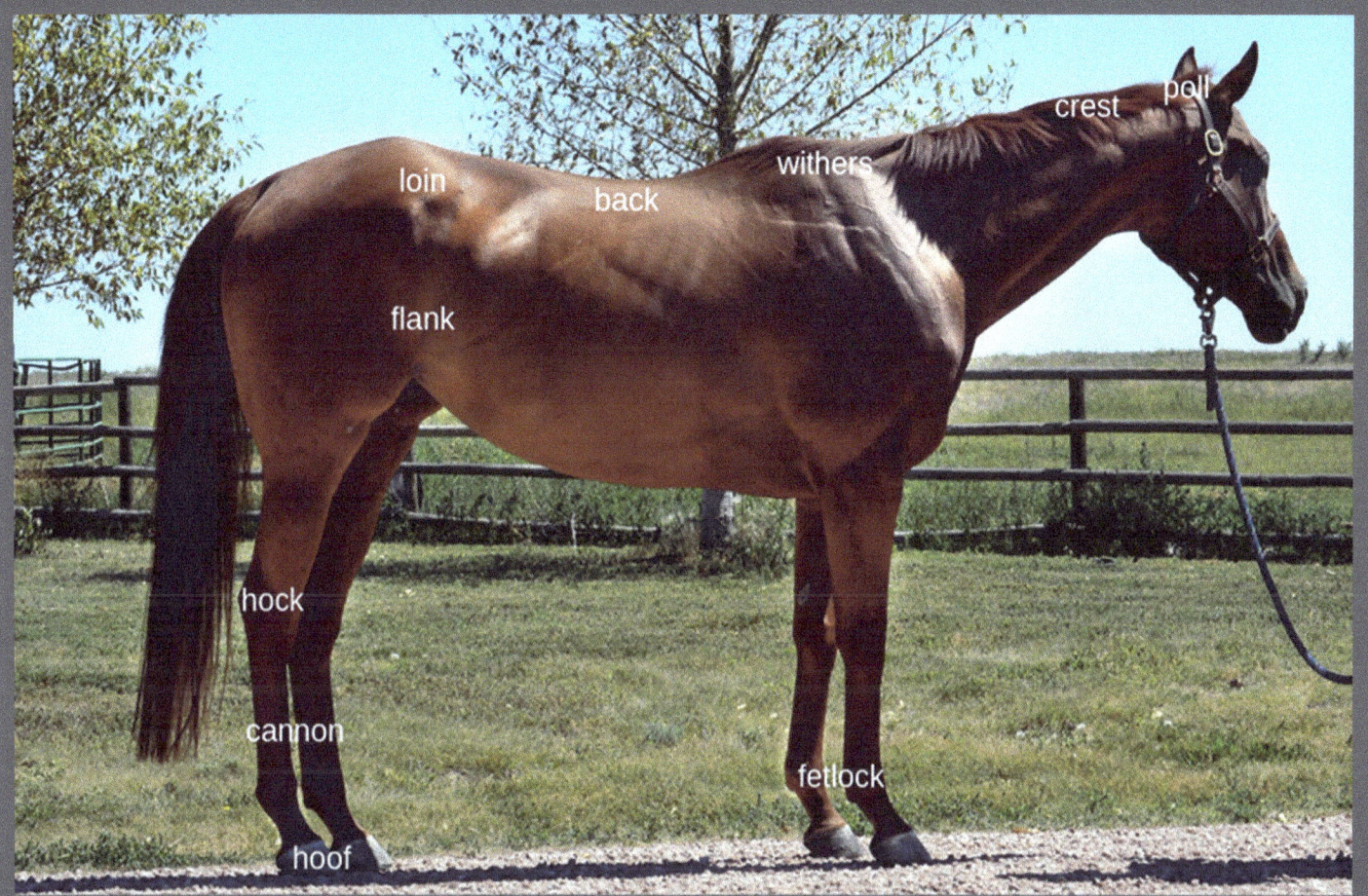

C is for conformation

Conformation is the appearance of the horse's body including bones and muscle.

D is for draft horse

Draft horses have wide bodies and big muscles so they can pull heavy loads.

E is for equestrian

An equestrian is a fancy name for a horseback rider or performer.

F is for foal

Foal is a term for any horse up to one year old.

F is for filly

A filly is a young female horse under four years old.

G is for gray

A gray refers to the color of coat ranging from white to dark gray. The shade of gray can change with the seasons.

A dapple gray has white circular markings.

G is for grullo

Grullo, also known as grulla, is characterized by tan-gray or mouse colored hair.

H is for haflinger

A haflinger is a small, draft horse.

I is for incisors

Humans have incisors as well. Unlike humans though, horses' teeth continue to grow throughout their entire lives. That's where the phrase "long in the tooth" comes from.

J is for jockey

A jockey is a person who rides in horse races.

J is for jumper

A jumper is a horse that is bred and trained to jump high.

K is for Knabstrupper
kah-nab-strooper

From Denmark, the Knabstrupper is well-known for its head to toe leopard pattern.

L is for lope
A horse's slow run is called a lope and makes the sound of three quick drum beats.

L is for lead
Horses are taught to follow with the help of a halter and lead rope.

M is for mane

The mane is the hair that grows from the top of the neck to the withers. It protects the neck from insects and helps drain off water.

M is for mule

A mule is the offspring of a female horse and male donkey.

N is for near side

Riders traditionally mount a horse on the left side, or near side.

O is for oats

Oats are a high energy food for horses. They gobble it up because of the sweet taste. Even horses want a tasty treat.

P is for paint

The American paint horse is known for its unique, beautiful markings.

P is for palomino

A palomino is a golden or tan colored horse with a white mane and tail.

P is for Percheron

The Percheron is a large draft horse, usually gray or black in color. They originated from France and are known for their intelligence and willingness to work.

P is for pony

A pony is a small horse under 4 feet 10 inches tall. What they lack in size, they make up for in energy and attitude.

Q is for quarter horse

A quarter horse is an American breed that excels at sprinting short distances.

bay roan

blue roan

strawberry roan

R is for roan

A roan has a mixture of colored and white hair.

S is for sorrel

Sorrel is a copper-red colored horse.

T is for thoroughbred

Thoroughbred is a breed of horse which is commonly used in horse racing.

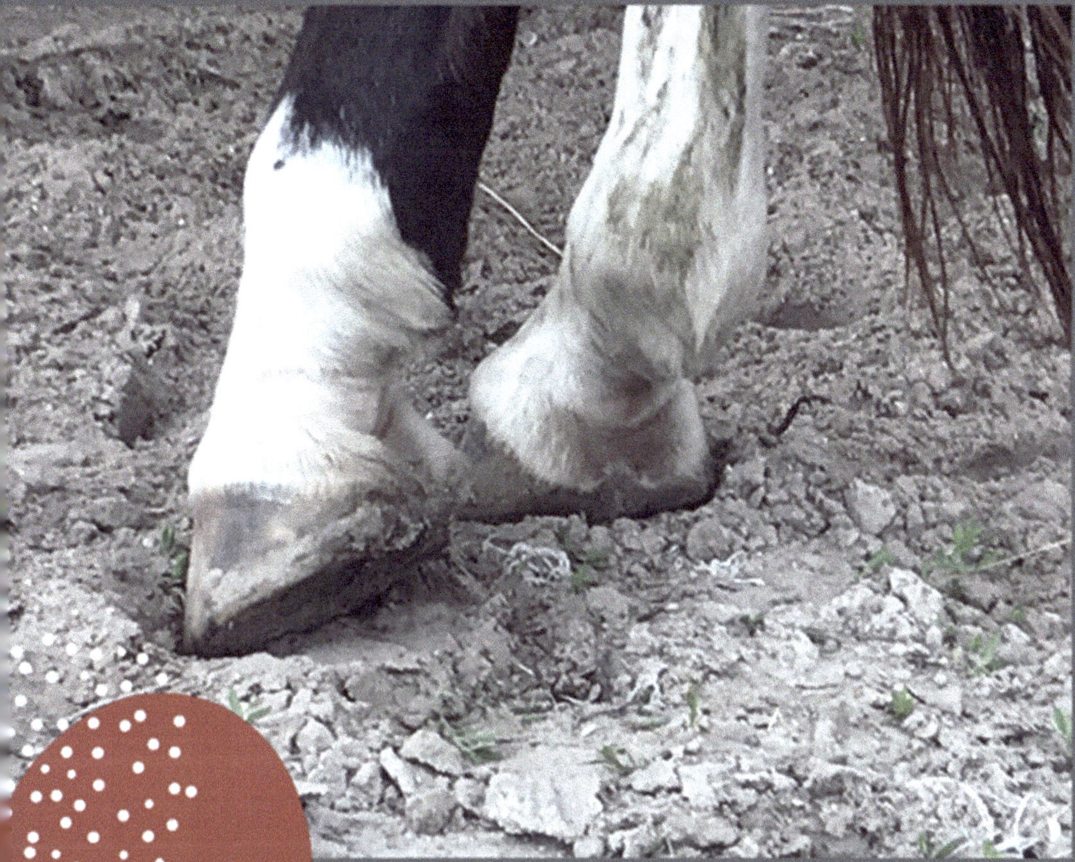

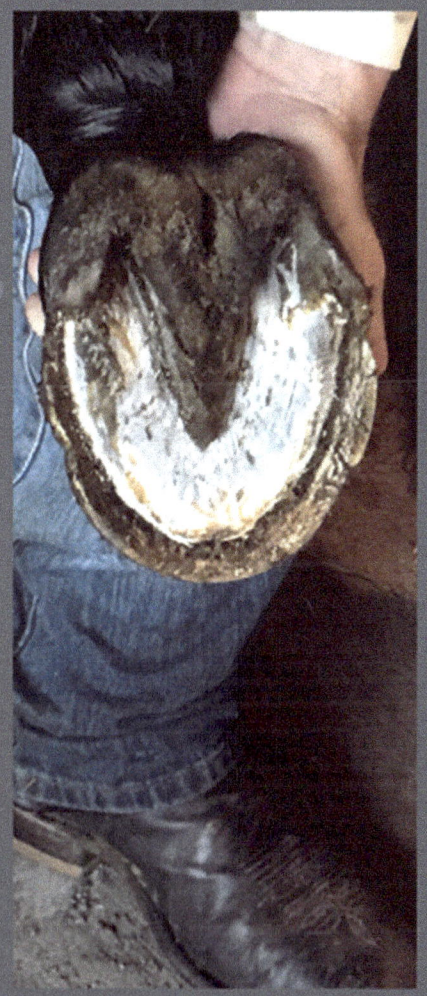

U is for unshod

Horses do not always require shoes. When possible, a barefoot or unshod hoof is a healthy option.

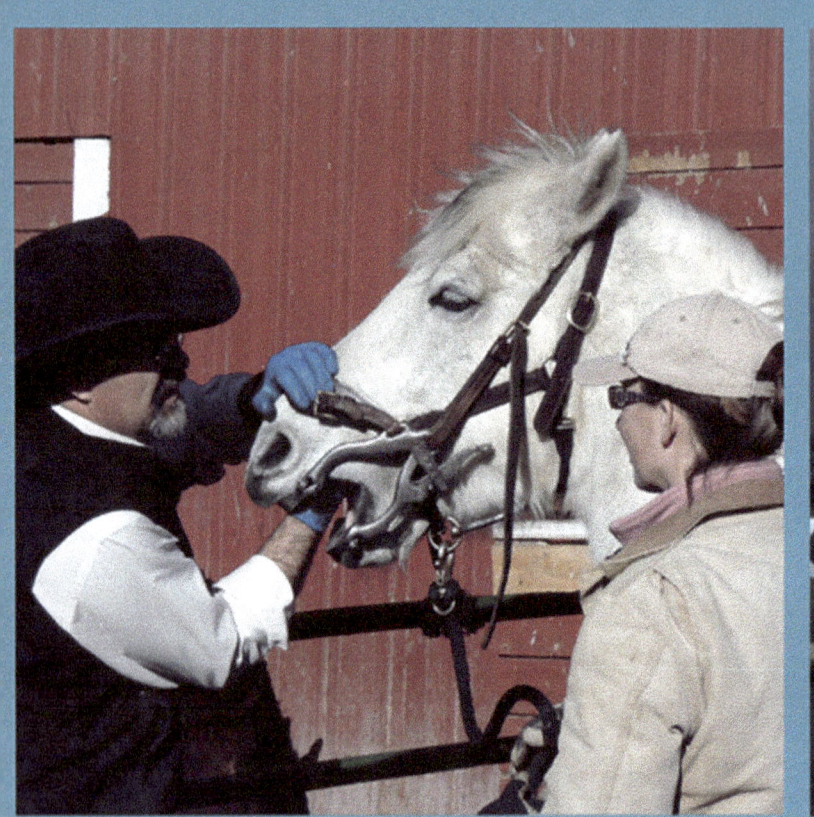
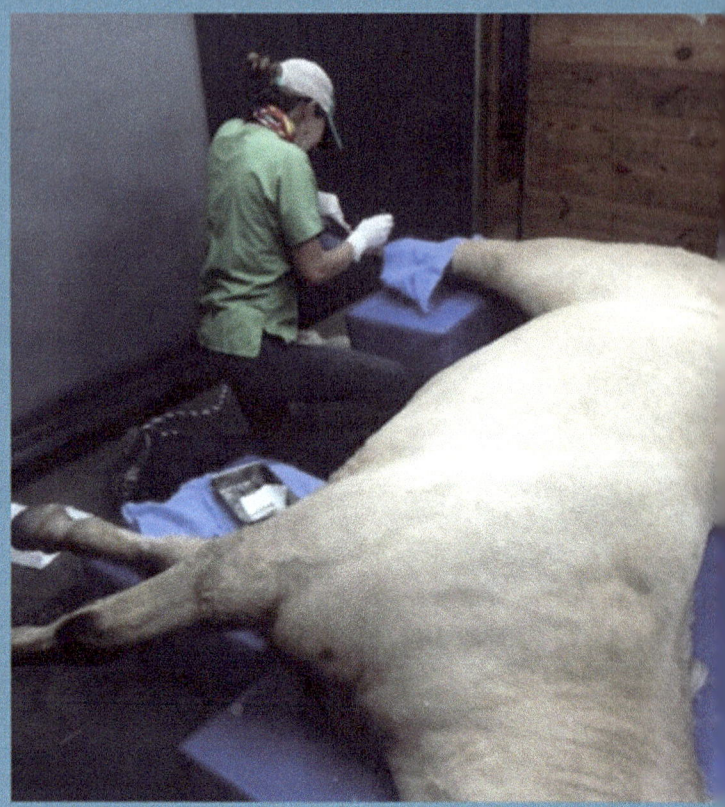

V is for veterinarian

A veterinarian is a doctor that cares for animals. Some veterinarians may specialize in large animals, such as horses.

W is for withers

>>>————————<<<

The withers are the highest part of the back at the base of the neck. A horse's height is measured from the ground to the withers and is measured in "hands." One "hand" is equal to four inches.

W is for winter coat

>>>————————<<<

When the daylight hours shorten, horses begin to grow longer hair known as their winter coats.

X is for eXercise

Horses need exercise such as jumping, running, and racing to keep their heart healthy and muscles strong.

Y is for yearling

A yearling is a horse that is between one and two years old.

Z is for zorse

A zorse is a crossbreed between a male zebra and a female horse. They usually maintain their wild instincts and are not considered tame animals.

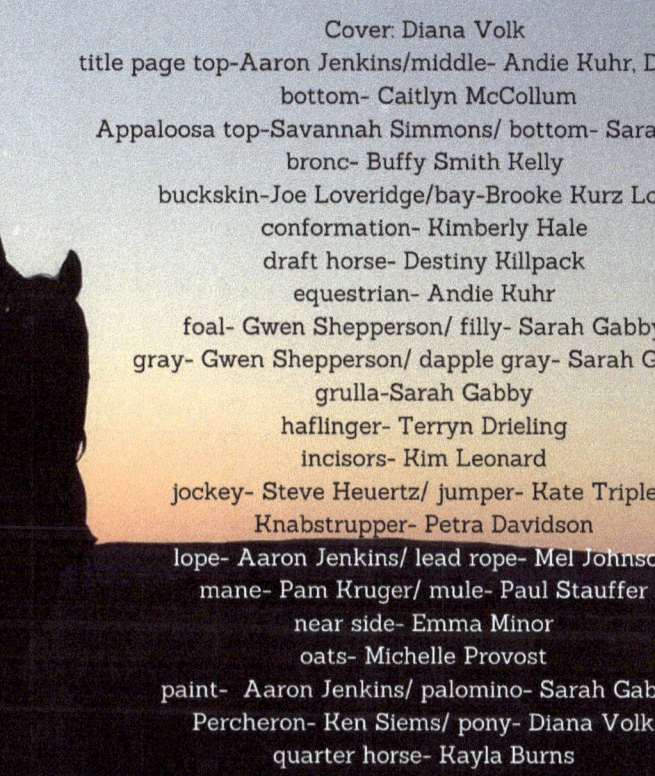

Cover: Diana Volk
title page top- Aaron Jenkins/middle- Andie Kuhr, Diana Volk
bottom- Caitlyn McCollum
Appaloosa top- Savannah Simmons/ bottom- Sarah Gabby
bronc- Buffy Smith Kelly
buckskin- Joe Loveridge/ bay- Brooke Kurz Lopez
conformation- Kimberly Hale
draft horse- Destiny Killpack
equestrian- Andie Kuhr
foal- Gwen Shepperson/ filly- Sarah Gabby
gray- Gwen Shepperson/ dapple gray- Sarah Gabby
grulla- Sarah Gabby
haflinger- Terryn Drieling
incisors- Kim Leonard
jockey- Steve Heuertz/ jumper- Kate Triplett
Knabstrupper- Petra Davidson
lope- Aaron Jenkins/ lead rope- Mel Johnson
mane- Pam Kruger/ mule- Paul Stauffer
near side- Emma Minor
oats- Michelle Provost
paint- Aaron Jenkins/ palomino- Sarah Gabby
Percheron- Ken Siems/ pony- Diana Volk
quarter horse- Kayla Burns
roan- (bay and strawberry) Kayla Burns / blue roan- Pam Kruger
sorrel- Aaron Jenkins
unshod- Michelle Provost
veterinarian- L to R - Kimberly Hale, Candice Carden
withers- Sarah Gabby/ winter coat- Amie Zanone
eXercise- top left Kimberly Hale top right- Diana Volk
bottom left- Sarah Gabby bottom right- Aaron Jenkins
yearling- Jecca Ostrander
zorse- Christa Leste-Lasserree

Copyright © 2019 by Michelle Provost

All rights reserved.

Published by ABC Fun Books

www.ABCFunBooks.com

mprovost2020@gmail.com

This book or any portion thereof may not be reproduced or used in any manner whatsoever without the express written permission of the publisher except for the use of brief quotations in a book review.

Printed in the United States of America

Second Edition

First Printing 2017